AF429010

Copyright © 2023 Dr. Isaiah Varisano

I'M GRATEFUL

Dr. Isaiah Varisano

I'm
grateful

for the bed that I
wake up in.

I'm
grateful

for the people who
wake me up.

I'm grateful

for toys to play
with.

I'm
grateful

for friends.

I'm
grateful

for the fun that I have.

I'm
grateful

that I have food to
eat.

I'm grateful

that I can learn
new things.

I'm
grateful

that stories are read
to me.

I'm grateful

for the bed that I
sleep in at night.

I'm
grateful

for you.

Benefits of Gratitude

Gratitude is the state of being thankful. Gratitude can also be a practice of noticing and appreciating the good things in your life. Decades of research on gratitude has shown that practicing and receiving gratitude has many potent benefits. Gratitude reduces pain, stress, anxiety, depression, and aggression. Gratitude improves physical health, relationships, resilience, self-esteem, sleep, decision making, job satisfaction, prosocial behavior, academic performance, immune response, emotional intelligence, and more. Learning to practice gratitude will benefit children and caregivers for the rest of their lives.

Tips for Cultivating Gratitude

- **Model Gratitude:** Babies and young children learn by observing, so parents and caregivers can set a positive example by expressing gratitude and appreciation regularly.

- **Use Positive Language:** Incorporate positive and appreciative language into your daily interactions with your children.

- **Practice Kindness:** Encourage acts of kindness and sharing from an early age. Show your child how to share toys, food, or affection with others.

- **Gratitude Rituals:** Create rituals that involve gratitude. For example, during mealtime or bedtime, you can express gratitude for the food you eat, the time you spend together, the positive moments in the day, etc. Most benefits of gratitude come from continued regular practice.

- **Celebrate Special Moments:** Make a big deal out of special moments and milestones in your baby's life. Celebrate birthdays, first steps, or other achievements to instill a sense of appreciation.